we love you

£7.99

© 2011. Published by Pillar Box Red Publishing Ltd.

Photography © Shutterstock.com

ISBN: 978-1-907823-15-2

we love you... Westie

PBR

A Pillar Box Red Publication

Written by Sarah Delmege
Designed by Jane Greig

Contents

we love you Westie because....

...You don't realize you're a dog!

...You are the most loyal friend we could ever have!

...You love us as much as we love you!

...You are a bundle of energy!

...You have a brilliant sense of fun!

...You cover us with doggy kisses!

...You are the cutest dog EVER!

Is A Westie Right For You?

So, what's it really like to live with a Westie? If any experienced Westie owner had to come up with a one-word answer to that question, the word would have to be FUN. Westies approach life and the world with a happy, light-hearted attitude that is one hundred per cent contagious.

Where can they live?

They are ideal pets for the town or the country. To a Westie, the number one priority is to be close to the people he loves best. That also means a Westie is a dog for the whole family. They can rough and tumble with the best of them and can be quiet and peaceful.

Westie Personality

If you are considering a Westie pet, then make sure you like pups with an active, get-up-and-go attitude. Westies have an awful lot of energy and they are incredibly vocal. Not surprising when you think they were originally bred to hunt and kill game and vermin in the rugged Scottish Highlands. Westies need very little encouragement to express their opinion about things! Of course this means that a Westie is usually a very keen watchdog. His size rules out his effectiveness as a guard dog (though not in his opinion!) but that loud bark is often enough to put off any intruder!

Exercise

Even though a Westie is small he loves being on the go. A Westie should have several good walks on-lead every day. Walking on a leash provides rhythmic exercise for your dog and is good for you too! Your Westie will also love to have you throw a favourite toy for him to catch and bring back for another throw.

How To Prepare For Your Westie Puppy

The needs of Westie puppies are not huge, but there are a few things you must have in place to give your Westie a safe, happy transition into your life.

It's much easier and safer to prevent your West Highland Terrier pup from getting into and destroying things than it is to watch him every second. Remember that any item they chew on is also an item that is potentially swallowed: bits of cloth, tassels, string and of course, shoes.

Make sure you secure everything that your pup could pick up or move. Electrical cords are a particular danger. A solution called 'bitter apple' can be sprayed on cords and anything else that can't be relocated, to discourage chewing.

Dog trainers recommend that you never give your new puppy the freedom to roam the house while you are gone. A crate will keep your dog secure. Make sure you pick one that is big enough for your pup to stand up and turn around in. Pet gates will keep it confined to a room of the house that has a durable floor. Since your Westie will not be old enough for reliable West Highland Terrier training until about four months of age, this will be essential if you want to keep your carpets stain free!

Your Westie dog will need to eat, so it's a good idea to ask the breeder what he has been eating and buy that brand. You can change the food later, but in the beginning your pup will have enough adjustments to make without a change in diet. It's a good idea to make sure your food and water bowls are made from stainless steel – your Westie will chew anything plastic.

To encourage your pup to chew on acceptable items have a selection of sturdy chew toys on hand.

You will want to get your Westie used to a collar and leash as quickly as possible. Buy a light collar and leash, suitable for puppies and get an ID tag to go with them.

The grooming routine is also something that your pup needs to experience as early as possible. Have a brush or comb ready at hand. Some owners recommend a bed of old towels or faux lambskin. Like everything else you buy for your Westie puppy, whatever you choose for a bed should be both washable and durable, as well as comfortable for your dog.

Last, but definitely not least, find a vet. A good West Highland White Terrier breeder will even let you bring the dog to a vet before you buy so you can make sure the dog you bring home is healthy.

How To Train Your Westie

Training is a great bonding experience for you and your new Westie. Plus, it isn't hard to train your Westie, since all he wants to do is please you!

1 Training is essential for every dog and can begin as early as eight weeks of age. Time spent teaching your Westie obedience skills should be fun and will establish a special loving bond between you and your dog.

2 Locate a reputable dog-training club, school or private obedience instructor. Ask your vet or breeder if they can recommend anyone.

3 Remember dog training should NEVER rely on force.

4 Praise, praise, praise when your Westie does what you want.

5 Be consistent and confident. Share your training programme with your family. One person should do most of the training.

6 Make sure you balance regular sessions of attention, affection, training and play. Twenty minutes of training a few times a week will keep you and your Westie motivated and interested in learning.

Top tip!
Make sure you praise and pet your puppy a lot, especially for a job well done. Don't forget to give yourself a pat on the back too!

7 Make sure your Westie learns the five basic training commands: sit, stay, heel, down and come. A well-behaved dog is welcome everywhere!

8 Training requires time and patience, but you will be rewarded by a Westie that is an absolute pleasure to live with!

we love you...

Things to Make For Your Westie

Dynamic Collar

Your Westie will look dashing in this designer collar – designed by you!

Get Ready!

- Nylon dog collar
- Ribbons (same width as the collar)
- Tape measure or ruler
- Hook-and-loop fastener tape with peel-and-stick backing
- Scissors
- Clear nail varnish
- A nail

Step-by-step

1. Measure the collar from end to end. Cut a piece of ribbon 7.5 cm longer than your measurement and apply clear nail varnish to the ends to keep them from unraveling. Allow to dry.
2. Hook-and-loop tape comes in strips, one for the 'hook' side and one for the 'loop' side. Cut small pieces of the tape to match the width of your collar.
3. Stick one of the 'loop' pieces about 2.5cm from the end. Add 'loop' pieces every 7.5cm to 10cm in between on the smooth side of the collar.
4. Turn the collar over and put one 'loop' piece about 5cm to 7.5cm in from the end of the collar, then turn the collar back over.
5. Set the ribbon, wrong side up beside the collar and attach one 'hook' piece of tape to the wrong side of the ribbon to match each 'loop' piece on the collar, including the one on the other side near the end of the collar.
6. Wait a few hours to make sure the hook-and-loop tape is firmly stuck to the collar and ribbon, then attach the ribbon by connecting the hook-and-loop pieces together.
7. You'll need to use a nail or another sharp object to poke holes in the ribbon in the spots where the collar has holes. If the holes close up (this happens with some ribbon), you can cut a slightly larger hole with scissors and apply clear nail varnish around its edges.

Luxury Fur Lined Dog Bed

Every Westie loves to sleep and your dog will adore this comfy bed!

Get Ready!
- 1.2m x 60 cm of fake fur
- 40cm x 60cm of any other thick fabric
- scissors
- large needle and thread
- old bath towel
- pins
- marker
- 30-40cm foam circle (for the bed's base)

Step-by-step!
1. Using the marker, draw around the foam circle at one end of each piece of fabric. Now, cut out the two circles leaving an extra 2cm all round for a hem.
2. Pin the circles together, fur side facing in, and then sew around, leaving a 15cm gap. Take out the pins as you sew.
3. Turn the circles inside out so that the fur is showing. Stuff the foam circle inside and sew up the gap. This is the bed's base.
4. From the remaining fur fabric, cut two 75cm by 30cm rectangles. Sew them together at one short end and fold lengthwise, fur side facing in. Sew along the length and turn right side out, so you have a long 1.5m x 15cm furry tube. This will form the sides of your Westie's bed.
5. Fold the towel until it fits snugly inside the tube.
6. Wrap the tube around the circular pillow so there are no gaps. Then pin and sew the edges together.
7. Sew the pillow and the sides together to finish off the bed!

Puzzle Fun

Are you as super-sharp as your Westie pup?
Test your skill on these puzzles.

Help Westie!

This cute pup needs to make it back through the maze to his owner. Can you help him?

Start

Finish

Pup Search

```
V C E P D T D L Q K H B G B W
U U D I O G A G D A E E N U F
R T T Y T Y J L K F E V I I P
S E I R O S I Q R O A S V A X
Z A V L P Q E A E W L A O W V
Y F R V F C T W H H C W L A F
X G N X J R H I T L Q Y A H U
G N I N I A R T S D G K Q L D
P D Z Q V O U L Z T R P O L K
R S B L I Z Q Q B A B C S D W
N I Y V U H A T W T Z I A X T
I E E C E M B G M I N E D J O
P K B C Q O B Z O J J I U B J
E D U D D J U H S Z E P L D A
J N A J B A R K S R G T F E V
```

BARK   FUN   LOYAL   TOY   WALK

CUTE   LOVING   SIT   TRAINING   WESTIE

Shadow Show

Which shadow matches this Westie pup perfectly?

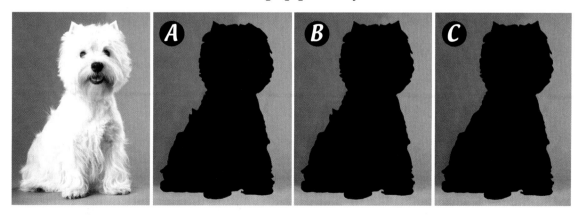

Westie Heroes

They may be small but Westies aren't afraid to step up to the plate! Check out these four-legged heroes.

Life Saver

When Mrs Clarke had a heart attack, Angus' relentless barking alerted neighbour Susan Green who rushed out and dialled 999 for help. When paramedics arrived they told her that she would have died if it hadn't been for the alert sounded by her Westie.

See You Later Alligator

Gary Murphy saved his pup, Doogie, from an alligator that had the West Highland Terrier locked in its mouth, by punching the six-foot beast on top of its head. Mr Murphy was working on a boat at his home in Palm City, Florida when the alligator made a play for his pooch, Doogie. He promptly launched himself on to the reptile's back, forcing the alligator to let go of a very relieved Doogie.

"I wasn't trying to be a hero, I just wanted my dog back," said the builder.

Canine Carer

A West Highland terrier has been dubbed a canine carer after giving a lonely and housebound pensioner a new lease of life. Mrs Davis had become nervous about leaving her home after suffering a fall. She was doing little during the day and felt very lonely. Ever since Digger started visiting twice weekly with his owner, Stan, Mrs Davis' confidence has improved in leaps and bounds and she now goes out shopping and visits the park! All thanks to her Westie pal.

Hero Hound

A tiny Westie was hailed a hero after saving his owner from her blazing flat. Sam woke his owner, Greta, as smoke filled her flat in Maidenhead by pawing her face as she slept. The hero hound had only lived with Mrs Broadley for eight days after she adopted him. "There is no doubt the dog saved her life," said the Fire and Rescue Service. Greta thanked the little dog with a slap-up chicken and tuna meal!

Win Your Own Westie

We have up for grabs a lovable, cuddly Westie that could be your very own. He requires very little maintenance and will arrive at your home already house-trained. A perfect pal for playtime and bedtime.

Just email a short story (500 words or fewer) about your Westie or a Westie you know and our favourite tale will receive this soft toy from Laura Ashley. Send your stories to enquiries@pillarboxredpublishing. co.uk with WESTIE COMPETITION as the subject. Please supply your name, address and contact telephone number.
Closing date: 31 January 2012.

Westie Competition terms and conditions

1. No purchase necessary.
2. The competition is open to all ages, professions and nationalities.
3. All entries must be original prose of 500 words or fewer.
4. Entrants may submit one entry only.
5. Entries must be submitted via email to enquiries@pillarboxredpublishing. co.uk with the subject heading: WESTIE COMPETITION. Please include your email address in the file if submitting as an attachment, or in the body of the email.
6. The closing date for entries is 31 January 2012. Entries will not be accepted after that date.
7. By submitting an entry all entrants thereby grant Pillar Box Red Publishing the right to publish their entry in future publications in the event of their entry being shortlisted and/or winning the competition.
8. Pillar Box Red Publishing cannot accept responsibility for entries which are not received or which are received after the closing date due to technical failure or for any other reason.
9. Pillar Box Red Publishing reserves the right to change the rules of this competition without notice.
10. The winner of the competition will be notified in February 2012.
11. The decision of the competition judges will be final and no correspondence will be entered into.
12. Employees of Pillar Box Red Publishing, and members of their immediate family, are excluded from participating in the competition.
13. The prize is a soft toy and not a real dog.

Spot The Difference!

Take a close look at these two pictures and see if you can spot all 5 differences between them.

we *love* you...

Caring For Your Westie

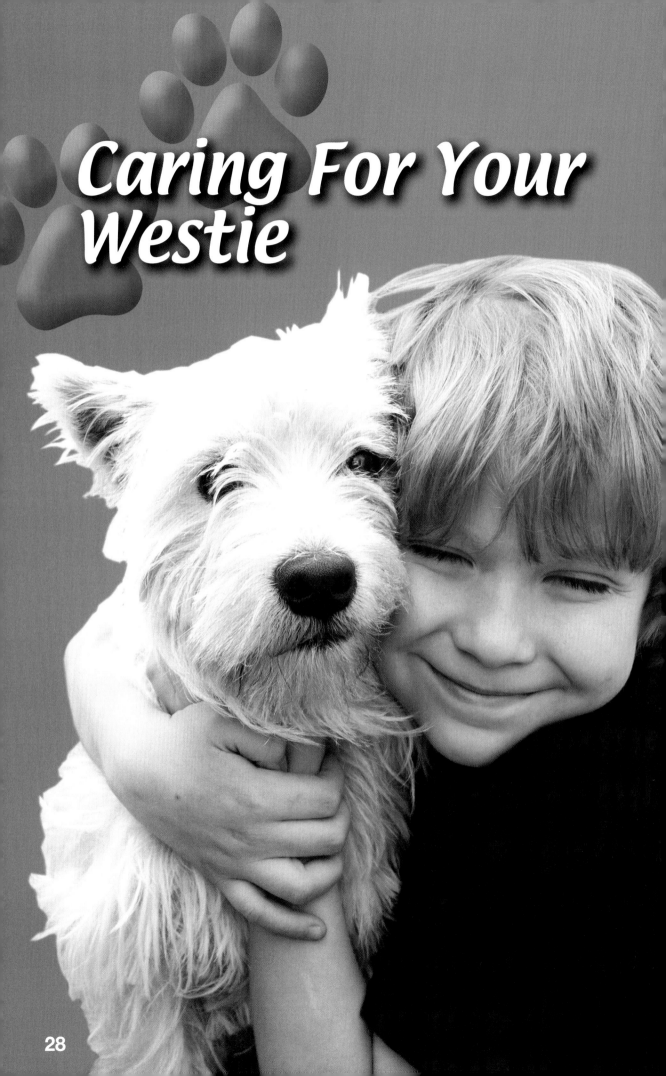

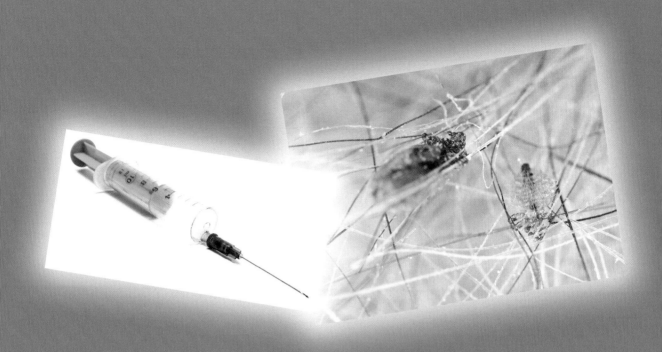

1. VACCINATIONS. The first and foremost thing that you should do is to get hold of a vaccination schedule. A good vet will advise you about vaccinations and what to look out for.

2. CHECK UPS. Despite sometimes having all the required certificates and credentials, your pup may still develop diseases and allergic reactions, so you should make sure your dog has a check up at least once a year.

3. GROOMING. These dogs need little, but regular grooming. Their coat is dry so it can look as good as new with a little brushing. Sometimes it's a good idea to have the hair trimmed in the popular lion style.

4. CLAWS. The grooming of claws should be done once a month if your Westie is very active outdoors.

5. CLEANING OF THE EARS. A Westie's ears attract a lot of dust because they are short and standing. They need to be cleaned on a monthly basis to prevent infection.

6. BATH. You'll only need to bathe your Westie once every couple of months. You'll need a good soap, a good shampoo and conditioner to soften the outer coat.

7. REGULARLY CHECK FOR PARASITES. There are many places where parasites can hitch a ride. Some of the favourite spots are behind the ears, under the muzzle, right under the arms, inside the ears, on the inside of the thighs and in between the toes.

Fascinating Facts

 The Westie is famous for his white face and sparkly eyes.

 Developed in Argyllshire in the Scottish Highlands, Westies were originally put to work as vermin hunters and exterminators.

 The Westie is one of the Scottish breeds of Terriers and comes from the same family group as the Cairn Terrier and Scottish Terrier.

 The Westie is double-coated. His two-inch outer coat is straight and harsh to the touch, which protected him from bad weather when he hunted.

 The Westie is mischievous, affectionate, devoted and extremely smart.

 West Highland Terriers can detect movement at a greater distance than we can, but they can't see as well up close.

 Westies are omnivorous – which means they eat meat as well as vegetables.

 You can count on a Westie to bring love, happiness and friendship into your home whenever you need it the most!

 A Westie's nose is his greatest sensory organ.

How To Throw Your Westie A Party

Before The Party

1. Write your guest list.
2. Make some invitations and pass them out to your friends. Don't forget the time, date and place where the party is being held.

On The Day of The Party

GARDEN

1. Check that the gate is closed and there are no holes in the fence.
2. Have shovels or bags on hand to pick up any messes when they happen.
3. Put any delicate flowerpots in the garage.
4. Have enough balls and dog toys available.

During The Party

1. If any presents are opened, throw away all wrapping paper, ribbons and bows straight away where the dogs can't reach them and eat them.
2. Think of some fun doggy games like relay races, hide and seek and hide the treats.
3. Get disposable cameras and give them to your friends so they can have souvenirs of all the fun.

Make a delicious cake for your Westie.

WHAT YOU NEED:

- 3 tins of dog food
- sausages
- large bowl
- bacon
- dog treats
- plate

WHAT TO DO:

- Empty the three tins of dog food into a bowl. Place it in the fridge overnight to set.
- Cook the sausage and bacon and leave overnight to cool.
- The next day, take the bowl of dog food out of the fridge, place the plate on top of the bowl and, turning it over carefully, empty out the contents. It should have set into the bowl's shape.
- Now take the sausages and place them right around the sides of the cake.
- Take the bacon and arrange it on top of the cake.
- Finally take the dog treats and use them to spell out your dog's name. And there you have it, a cake fit for your best canine friend.

we love you...

Westies On TV

Thanks to their friendly temperaments and movie star good looks, Westies have gone on to become famous actors, starring in film and television, as well as models and characters of books. Here's some of them.

M& S Advert

Two adorable East Sussex Westies went from being down and out to enjoying television fame after being chosen to star in a Marks and Spencer advert – alongside top models including Twiggy and Lisa Snowdon.

Life wasn't looking great for West Highland terriers Alfie and Izzy when their owner died and they found themselves at the Blue Cross animal charity adoption centre in Northiam, looking for a new home.

But just a few months later, things were looking up. Not only do Alfie and Izzy have a loving new home but a TV appearance under their collars.

They 'auditioned' for the advert and made the grade along with 18 other dogs and went off to London for a day of filming and star treatment.

Cesar

Cesar is the mascot and poster dog for Cesar brand dog food. The Westie that appears in the ads is named Maggie.

King Of The Hill

On the cartoon series *King of the Hill*, Doggy, the pet of the Souphanousinphone family is a Westie.

Greyfriars Bobby

The book *Greyfriars Bobby* by Eleanor Atkinson, told the true story of a Skye Terrier that spent the better part of his life sitting on his master's grave. In the film of the book, *The Adventures of Greyfriars Bobby*, Bobby was portrayed by a West Highland White Terrier.

Can you think of any other famous Westies?

Westie Travel Tips

Taking your Westie with you on holiday or on an outing can be great fun for both of you, provided you have it carefully planned. Here are the things you should think about.

Will your Westie travel with you in car, train, boat or plane? Each method of transport has its own rules, so make sure you check them out before you leave.

How are you travelling?
Travel can be tiring and your dog should be in good health to deal with new or stressful situations. Make sure your Westie is wearing a collar with his ID.

The age of your Westie
Is your pet a small puppy or an older dog? Puppies need to relieve themselves more frequently and need more attention, which might be more difficult. Though they need

more sleep than an adult, keeping them shut in a crate all day long isn't the best choice. You might want to avoid travelling with them until they are around 6 months old. The same can be said for old dogs who have difficulty adapting to changes in their lifestyle, develop a lot of stress and who are better left at home.

His health condition

In general, injured or sick Westies shouldn't travel. This is especially true if you can't keep an eye on them all the time or if the trip is going to last more than a few hours. Before taking a trip always make sure your Westie is healthy with up-to-date vaccinations.

His temperament

Think twice before you bring a Westie who vocalizes a lot, is grumpy, unruly or not housetrained. Also think about the level of anxiety he experiences when he's away from you and the way he reacts with a pet sitter or when boarded. If in doubt, you can try it for a day or two and get your dog used to the situation gradually.

Will your Westie have a chance to enjoy the trip?

Do you intend to travel for only two or three hours at a time? Or do you intend to travel for long distances every day? If you will be city visiting and your Westie lives in the country and is used to running freely in his garden, he won't be happy if your trip doesn't allow for some doggy activities where he can enjoy himself and have fun too.

Where are you staying?

The decision to bring the dog or not will be very different depending on whether you're staying with friends or family, in a hotel or going camping. Don't forget to mention you will be travelling with a dog and enquire whether there are any special fees or conditions.

Other options

You might be lucky enough to have a friend, family member or neighbour who will be happy to stay at your place and do some pet sitting or will keep your dog at their place. While you will miss your pup on holiday, this is often the best solution. The next best option is to have a reliable pet sitter who will feed and walk your Westie at least twice a day.

Decisions Decisions

When you make your decision, you have to consider whether your Westie will have fun with you on holiday. Include walks in your daily schedule. Even better, bring him to the country where he can discover different sights and new smells. There's nothing more fun than seeing a bright-eyed Westie tail up, and ears erect when his curiosity is aroused. So don't forget your camera!

Easy Tips for Westie Grooming

Learning how to groom a Westie is key to making this lovable breed look its best.

1 Begin to get your Westie used to being groomed by brushing him or her frequently – starting at a young age.
This will not only adapt your pet to regular dog grooming but will keep the coat looking fresh between baths and trims.

2 Trim the hair around your Westie's eyes and ears.
This dog-grooming tip should be performed with blunt tip scissors or clippers. Be very careful not to cut your Westie's skin.
This should be done about every 4 months.

3 Cut your Westie's nails.
This is best done with dog toenail clippers or scissors.
As with all dog-grooming tips, start cutting your Westie's nails when he's young – to avoid fear of nail trimming later.

4 Give your Westie a bath.
As you learn how to groom your Westie you will realize your pet doesn't need a bath too frequently when brushed regularly. This is because a Westie's coat doesn't tend to trap dirt when neatly groomed.

5 Continue to brush your Westie between trimmings and baths.
This will keep your Westie's coat and appearance in tip top shape!

Do

- Think about taking your Westie to a reputable professional groomer.
- When buying dog shampoo try to find one specifically for white coats. This will give your Westie's coat highlights and shine.

Don't

- Be harsh or rough when grooming your Westie.
- Get shampoo in his eyes.

Grooming checklist

- ☐ Dog shampoo
- ☐ Dog toenail clippers
- ☐ Blunt-tipped scissors
- ☐ Dog clippers or shears

Westie Quiz

1. Where did the Westie originally come from?
   a) Wales
   b) Scotland
   c) England
   d) Ireland

2. How long can a Westie live for?
   a) 7- 10 years
   b) 12-15 years
   c) 18-20 years
   d) 21 years or more

3. What must you never give your Westie?
   a) Chicken
   b) Chocolate
   c) A ball to play with
   d) Biscuits

4. If your Westie is unwell, take him to:
   a) Doctor
   b) Vet
   c) Animal Home
   d) Policeman

5. A lead is used to:
   a) Connect the radio to electricity
   b) Solve a crime
   c) Walk your dog
   d) Win a race

6. Westie belongs to a type of dog called:
   a) Terriers
   b) Poodles
   c) Wolves
   d) Hunting

7. Westies must be protected against:
   a) Worms
   b) Fleas
   c) Dog diseases
   d) All of these answers

8. Westie is short for:
   a) West Midlands
   b) West Country
   c) West Highland
   d) Westhampton

we ❤ love you...

Westie House Rules

House training requires persistence, dedication and an awful lot of repetition; it's so worth it when you show off your beautifully behaved Westie.

1   Keep your Westie confined in his crate when you cannot watch him. This includes during the night and when you are out. This is one of the most important rules of house training to abide by at all times. Dogs do not like to relieve themselves where they sleep, so crating your Westie when you are busy with other things will teach him to wait for you to take him out.

2   Watch your Westie closely to discover what type of signals he gives off before he piddles. Some puppies will begin to sniff the carpet frantically and others may begin to circle as they look for a spot to eliminate.

3   Open the crate door and take your Westie outside immediately when he wakes up in the morning or after daytime confinement. Having a routine will help with the house training process.

4   Take your Westie puppy outside to spend a penny every 10 minutes during playtime. Accidents can happen quickly in the middle of play, so you will need to be on your toes.

5   Catch your Westie in the act of widdling accidentally in the house in order for your efforts to be effective. Punishing after the fact does not work. The attention span of a puppy is so short that he will have long forgotten the accident by the time you scold him.

6   Guide your Westie to the door immediately after he drinks. If you give your puppy a big bowl of water after a long walk or play session, pay close attention. He will need to urinate within minutes, and if you miss his signals, you will miss another opportunity to house train him.

7   Walk your Westie after feeding time. Most Westies will need to pee 10 minutes after feeding and pass a bowel movement within 30-45 minutes of eating. So plan on taking your Westie for a long walk after feeding to teach him that outdoors is the place to eliminate after a meal.

NO PETS IN PLAY AREA

http://www.youtube.com/watch?v=DoKLR7ci9TE&feature=related
This little bundle of fluff is too scared to walk down the stairs!

Westie Puppies On The Web

Can't get enough cute Westie puppies?
Check out these sweeties...

http://www.youtube.com/watch?v=LSxgwCqMff0&feature=related
Possibly the cutest Westie EVER!

www.youtube.com/watch?v=T5VDmT7vPo4
This little Westie doesn't like strangers!

www.youtube.com/watch?v=x2-7_k9qHi4
Westie puppies playing.

www.youtube.com/watch?v=m0Mk9ZRIAgs
A litter of cuties playing in the garden.

www.youtube.com/watch?v=MewjCBSiFxA
It's a Westie in a box!

we *love* you...

Eye Spy!

Take a close look at these two pictures and see if
you can spot all 5 differences between them.

All About Westie

Sound

Westies, like all dogs can hear about four times better than we can and they can hear high-pitched sounds incredibly well.

Sight

Westies can detect movement at a greater distance than we can, but they can't see as well up close. They can also see better in less light, but can't distinguish many colours.

Taste

Westies have fewer taste buds than we do, so they're likelier to try anything – and usually do, which is why it's important for you to watch what they eat.

Smell

A West Highland Terrier's sense of smell is so great he can follow a trail that's weeks old, detect smells diluted to one-millionth the concentration we need to notice them and can even sniff out a person under water!

Touch

Westies are very social and love to be petted, groomed and played with.

My Westie

Fill in facts about your Westie
(or the Westie you wish you had!) here...

My Westie is called ....

Here is a picture of him/her

He/She is .... tall

He/She weighs ....

His/Her favourite thing to eat is ....

His/Her favourite place to be stroked is ....

He/She really loves chasing ....

The thing he/she love the most is ....

He/She really doesn't like ....

If I had to describe him/her in five words, I would say

1 ....

2 ....

3 ....

4 ....

5 ....

10 Tips For A Happy Life With A Westie

(according to your Westie!)

1 Stop thinking you're in charge. It's not true anyway and you are only making it all harder.

2 Not clear about your mission in life? Don't worry; you're here to make your Westie happy.

3 If you dream that someone is walking over you, it's not a dream, it's your Westie.

4 Everything valuable or everything he likes is his. You'd better give it to him at once.

5 Don't make any plans for a walk. It's not your walk anyway. Just follow your Master.

6 Your food is much dearer to him than you. Your Westie would happily swap you for a piece of bread.

7 Do you have a favourite chair? It's better you give it to him, before he has to take it from you.

8 Learn as much as you can about his body and personality and take proper care of him.

9 He's very intelligent, has a bright brain, and enjoys logical tasks. He never does anything chaotically, he thinks about everything he does and he's very goal-orientated and inventive.

10 Your Westie can give your life a completely different and new dimension. He'll help you grow and become an even better human being. In return help him develop his abilities, create a happy, healthy and loving home for him. He will love you for that.

Real Life Westies:
McKenzie

McKenzie has a very friendly and feisty nature – both classic attributes of the West Highland Terrier breed. Her owner, Suzanne Rendal, chose McKenzie from all the other puppies because she was so friendly and cute!

When pedigree puppies are born, they are given their official Kennel Club name. McKenzie's official name is Gabriella Whiteshine – as you can see she lives up to her pedigree name!

Suzanne loves to dress up McKenzie and she looks great in her outfits. McKenzie loves to be fussed over and models any coat or outfit with relish! She is always happy to sit on your lap and be pampered.

Every few weeks McKenzie gets groomed at the dog groomer's. She loves being pampered! Gillian the groomer says that McKenzie's favourite part is the shampooing because she loves the bubbles! She

always looks beautiful after being groomed and people tell her owner that she should be a dog model!

McKenzie is a very active dog because she goes to The Dog Day Care Centre four days a week! She spends all day playing with her doggie friends and goes for long country walks. She is always very tired when she gets home because of all the running about she has been doing with her doggie pals!

Suzanne says that McKenzie is a very special Westie, not just because of her wonderful personality, but also because of her big fluffy ears! Every time you talk to McKenzie her

ears spring up- which means she is definitely paying attention to you, unless of course she sees a squirrel – then she is off at a hundred miles an hour on a chase!

www.dogdaycarecentre.co.uk

57

Would You Like To Help A Westie?

Even if you don't own a Westie you can still help your four-legged pals.

Every year hundreds of Westies are rehomed through charities. There are a number of reasons why a dog needs to be rescued. The most common are:

• Long-term illness or death of an owner
• Change in accommodation – sometimes flats do not allow pets or aren't suitable
• Situations change
• Abandoned / Abused / Neglected

Charities like the Westie Rescue Scheme are dedicated to finding permanent homes for West Highland Terriers and offer help, advice and support on all Westie matters.

You can help them by joining as a 'Friend', through dog sponsorship or by shopping online.

Check out their website:
www.westierescuescheme.org.uk

Or you can contact the Dogs Trust Home
www.dogstrust.org.uk

Or the Blue Cross Animal Welfare Charity
www.bluecross.org.uk

Or D for dog charity
www.dfordog.co.uk

Or the PDSA
www.pdsa.org.uk

Quiz answers

Pup search

```
V C E P D T D L Q K H B G B W
U U D I O G A G D A E E N U F
R T T Y T Y J L K F E V I I P
S E I R O S I Q R O A S V A X
Z A V L P Q E A E W L A O W V
Y F R V F C T W H H C W L A F
X G N X J R H I T L Q Y A H U
G N I N I A R T S D G K Q L D
P D Z Q V O U L Z T R P O L K
R S B L I Z Q Q B A B C S D W
N I Y V U H A T W T Z I A X T
I E E C E M B G M I N E D J O
P K B C Q O B Z O J J I U B J
E D U D D J U H S Z E P L D A
J N A J B A R K S R G T F E V
```

Spot the Difference

Shadow Show

The matching shadow is B.

Westie Quiz

Answers
(from Page 42)

1. b) Scotland
2. b) 12-15 years
3. c) chocolate
4. b) Vet
5. c) Walk your dog
6. a) Terriers
7. d) All of these answers
8. c) West Highland

Eye spy!

we love you...

Where's Westie?